CASH $1000 in
24 Hours
From the **Internet**

The
Ultimate Guide

By Neslyn Watson-Druée

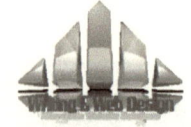

Published by WSDesgin.us - Publishing Department

Neslyn Watson-Druée - Beacon Organizational Development
CASH $1000 in 24 Hours from the Internet The Ultimate Guide
by Neslyn Watson-Druée

ISBN# 978-1-304-38709-7

Cover design by WSDesign.us - Web Design Division
Images from creative commons and Crestock Corp.
Interior architecture by WSDesign.us

Earnings Disclaimer

Contents

Yes You Can Generate Cash Fast

Do you sincerely want to generate cash quickly? What would you do if you needed $1000 - $2000 quickly, like in the next 24 hours? Do you know how or where you will get it? When unplanned expenses occur, and they do, are you prepared? *"How do I generate $1000 - $2000 in the next 24 hours?"* is the first questions asked by my students who attend my *Wealth Acceleration Blue Print* ™ Seminars. Students, who attend my seminars, all have one thing in common; the desire to be debt-free while building their entrepreneurial portfolio. They all want cash quickly to innovate and build their brand.

I have had times of pressing needs when I needed to generate cash fast and I have studied how to do so by following tried and tested steps of others who have successfully accomplished this task. I was able to take the steps of others and improve upon them with my own ideas. I have consistently achieved the desired results. My students have also achieved desirable results and now it is time for me to pass this information onto you. I am sharing my collective knowledge so that you too can have amazing results, if you take action and follow the steps and recommendations as detailed in this guide.

I have created a fool-proof system for becoming debt-free by generating cash quickly. As a result of frequent inquiry on how to generate cash fast, I will teach you the same steps that myself and my students have taken to achieve undeniable, proven results. Just owning and reading this guide is not enough to be successful. I want you to make the commitment to invest your time to follow through, take action on the steps and recommendations, track your progress and record your results.

Maybe you are, at this moment, needing fast cash to:
§ Invest in your business
§ Increase your income
§ Learn a new skill or acquire additional knowledge
§ Purchase a necessary item
§ Help a family member or a friend in need
§ Support activities in your local community

Perhaps, at present, you do not have the cash to meet your needs and desires. There are numerous so called experts, ranging from eBay arbitrage to Profit Loop system on the Internet, advocating various ways to make money fast and few can pass the test when asked to show proven, real life results.

I am reassuring you that I am practicing what I am preaching to generate $1000 or more in 24 hours, whenever I need to. Many of my students have taken action, implemented the steps and recommendations and, as a result, are now earning the money they need to achieve their goals. Like me and my students, **You too can generate cash fast** to meet your needs.

This guide is tried and tested and is backed by my personal experience. Simply put - It works when you step up and take action. The best guide in the world will not work for you unless you follow through.

"Do not wait to strike till the iron is hot; but make it hot by striking." ~William B. Sprague

If you are on this page with me, you may be asking yourself:

> "Is this another one of those unworkable schemes that I have read a hundred times before?"

I assure you, it isn't. Stay with me and follow on.......

Follow Me Upwards and Onwards...

Step-by-Step

I am making an assumption that you want to know how to generate some cash quickly, but you neither have a product to sell nor do you have customers to sell it to.

Is that right? Yes or No? If yes, this guide is for you.

Step 1 - Research

Begin by scanning online forums in your niche, such as Warrior, and The Internet Marketing Inner Circle (assuming that Internet marketing is your niche).

The Internet Marketing Inner Circle is open to "members only." However, membership is very affordable, and membership gives you access to some of the brightest marketing minds on this earth.

TIMIC Resource: http://bit.ly/18ccYwF

If you are not in the Internet marketing niche, look for forums in your niche. Simply type your keyword into your search bar, plus *forum* or *discussion board.*

Follow on by entering your keywords into the software, which will then point out top sites, you will notice that many of these sites have forums.

For example, if you typed in The Events Manager Forum you would be directed to site like;
http://the-emf.org.uk/

Events Management Forum - The site below highlight some discussions

http://forums.sforce.com/t5/Best-Practices-Discussion/Improving-event-management/td-p/27681

You are doing brilliant so far, you have started your research - When you visit the discussion forums you are at the beginning of your research. This means that you want to see what hot topics members of these communities might be willing to PAY for more information on. So, you want to scan forums looking for clues.

Look at what forum members are talking about. Many forums are set up to show you how many views and responses there are to each thread. Look for most viewed and most commented on threads. Just be sure they are active threads.

Continue your research by looking at the warrior Forum - Type *Internet Marketing Forum* into your browser and look in the results for: http://www.warriorforum.com

On The Warrior Forum, scan the Warrior Special Offers (WSO's), looking for most viewed, and most commented threads, as well as those with the most positive feedback. The Warrior Special Offers Forum is a place where members actually sell things to each other (at a special discount price). This will show you what types of products are popular sellers there.

Scan the Forums and look for the really pressing problem. By reading the threads of all the Forums, you are looking for an indicator of what is extremely painful to people, because people are happy to pay for product(s) that will end their pain. Remember people are motivated by two things, (1) by pleasure (2) by pain.

Note the problems which will enable you to put your ideas into action, by that I mean, you have ideas from which you can develop a simple, benefits-packed, information product. For example, I am thinking something like a special report that you can write quickly, and sell for $3 to $7.

Now you are looking for an indicator of a really hot topic, or some product (or product category) that is TRULY selling well within the Warrior Special Offers Forum.

I repeat - When reading the threads in all of the forums, what you're looking for is an indicator of extreme pain.

Where are people having the most pain? What ideas do you have that will enable and help people to solve their pain? People happily pay for products that end their pain.

Step 2 - Test the market

In advance of creating any product, **check** that it's something that is really wanted and something that people are already paying for.

My experience with clients tells me that the biggest mistake people make, when introducing new products to market, is that they do not test whether there is a market for their products. It does not matter how much you love your product, unless people are willing to pay for your product or idea, it simply doesn't matter. There is no value in producing products and services that are not in demand.

Get this idea firmly into your senses: *In creating a product, you don't have to start from scratch*. You could easily take one of the many products that you have Private Label Rights (PLR)to and quickly rework it, making sure that it is highly accurate, addresses a pressing need and contains some fresh, original content.

Most people with Private Label Rights products (PLR) fail to do anything with them, yet they are fairly easy to rework. Most of the work/research has been done with PLR products – so go the extra mile and make a new product. Most of the work has already been done for you. All you have to do is recycle, re-purpose and refresh.

Step 3 - Recycle, Re-Purpose and Refresh

All you really need to do to **have Fresh**, in-demand products with a Private Label Rights (PLR) package is:

1. Rework the copy, fix grammar and spelling errors, add your own affiliate links and add testimonials when you get them.

2. Add your own unique graphics if desired and change the title. Your goal in reworking a Private Label Rights product is to change it enough so that even owners of the original Private Label Rights product may not recognize it.

3. Read through the original product, make minor corrections and revisions where needed and add valuable content. Then rename it and put your name on it as the author, if you so desire.

4. Add text links in the content that take readers to associated affiliate products that you recommend and that would be of benefit to your readers. With many of these reworked PLR products, your links will ensure maximum profit.

5. As soon as you have your product completed, start marketing it immediately. Keep in mind that your goal is to make $1000 or even better in 24 hours or less.

That means that you need to spend more time "doing" than thinking about it.

Also, I recommend that you use reworked PLR products, as free products in list building giveaways. Participating in those free giveaways will add many new subscribers to your lists and auto-responders.

Remember, *The Money Truly IS In The List*, So your list will connect to an incredibly long-term income stream for you.

Step 4 - Unlock Your Product Success

The product that you produce has to make a **BIG** promise in how it will solve your potential customers' problems.

Dan S. Kennedy calls the type of advertisement that you use in selling your product, The Giant Promise. Your product (solution) must promise such amazing results that it borders on unbelievable, yet at the same time it must not be a false promise. This is a critical factor in how well your sales will go. The Giant Promise sells products like hot-chocolate.

Here are some examples of
The Giant Promise

§   Maybe you discovered a way to get listed at better than number one at Google. So you write a report on how to do that. Better than number one sounds almost impossible, but it can be done by using press releases. News stories and press releases are often listed above all else on the Search Engine Results Pages, even above sponsored listings.

§   Maybe you discovered a way to dramatically improve your ranking overnight. After verifying that it works every time or even the majority of the time, you document it by taking notes through every step. Then you can make that big claim in your promotions (perhaps with a small disclaimer).

§ You may have created a squeeze page template that consistently converts 80% of visitors into subscribers. You start marketing *The Amazing Squeeze Page Template* **Upheld** *To Convert 80% Of Site Visitors.*

At this point, it is important that you resist any negative self-talk. For example, *you may actually be saying to yourself, this is a lot of work*. Yes, it can be, but it doesn't have to be, especially if you start with a Private Label Rights product.

Regardless, if you really want to make $1000 or even better in the next 24 hours, you have to:

Eliminate all excuses and just create and market the product (the simplest of which is a short report).

Get it down on paper, and then you can go back and refine it several times.

> *"… years ago my older brother, who was ten years old at the time, was trying to get a report written on birds that he'd had three months to write, which was due the next day. We were out at our family cabin in Bolinas, and he was at the kitchen table close to tears, surrounded by binder paper and pencils and unopened books about birds, immobilized by the hugeness of the task ahead. Then my father sat down beside him put his arm around my brother's shoulder, and said, "Bird by bird, buddy. Just take it bird by bird."*
> **~Anne Lamott**

Get it down on paper, and then you can ask several

friends to review it for you and suggest changes. However, it's more important to get it written and into the marketplace than to make it perfect. As you roll it out, you may want to offer review copies to a few people for free reviews/testimonials. Based upon their feedback, you may improve upon the product, releasing an updated version at a later date.

At first you need to:
Focus on completion rather than perfection.

Your product does need to be accurate, deliver tremendous value and deliver all that you promised in your promotion. However, it does not need to be perfect.

When using Private Label Rights (PLR) products, it is vital that you confirm anything you proclaim your product can do. Test everything and confirm the absolute accuracy. When you don't confirm what your products teach, and blindly pass that on, you are setting yourself up for failure, loss of credibility and potential colossal refunds.

As you finish the product, one of the things to consider is pricing. *What you can get for your product depends upon perceived value.* However, for short, quick reports that you can generate in a short time, I recommend that you sell them at a low price. I have seen excellent results with the strategy of selling at a low price. Remember, your goal is $1000 or even better in 24 hours. So, again, you want the price to be so low that your potential customers realize their risk is almost none, but not so low that they will perceive it to have no value.

Price your report at $3 to $7, and I recommend that you use PayPal to process the orders. If you price the report at $7 and worded your **Giant Promise** promotion correctly, you should easily be able to sell the 150 copies you'd need to sell to raise the $1000 within 24 hours. My reason for 150 units rather than 143 is because you would have small PayPal fees. I have not calculated the precise PayPal fees, but rather rounded off the numbers to cover the expense.

Note the following:
The first glitch you might have is that with your first product, your mailing list might be small. If it's a small list, that is a legitimate concern, but also an excuse. Excuses only lead to failure. Your list will grow as long as you take the necessary steps to make it happen.
For inspiration, and ideas, check this blog post, *Earn over $1000 per day by writing.*
http://makealivingwriting.blogspot.co.uk/2013/04/how-to-make-1000-per-day-writing-what.html

Step 5 - Promoting your Product

If you have no list to begin with, be sure you have looked everywhere. Check your email contacts, Twitter, Facebook and other social sites you participate in. Still coming up short? Then you simply have to get creative, and use alternative promotion methods. There are many free and low-cost ways of marketing for you to get started with. All you need is determination and you will quickly be on your way to making $1000 cash in 24 hours.

7 Plan Quick Marketing System™

1. Write an advertisement as well as swap articles. Post ads to forums that have a free advertising section. Also send out press releases to promote your product.
2. Post your product on Discussion forums in your niche and create a few banners that include your "Giant Promise."
3. Buy solo advertisements and ask for recommendations on Twitter to further engage your followers.
4. Post your product on Twitter and ask your followers to re-tweet your post.
5. Visit popular blogs in your niche and comment on them. Whenever possible, leave a link to your product on Amazon or your sales page.
6. Blog about your product or special offer. Write an article on the central theme of your product and

post it on as many article directories as possible.

7. Ask Friends to send mailings for you. Maybe promise to mail for them after you have built your list.

One very good, low-cost marketing method is to open a fiverr.com account. You will find many workers on there who will tweet their very large lists for only five dollars. It is a great source of other marketing methods as well and a venue to ignite your creativity.

Step 6 - Product Sustainability Marketing 10 Tips™

(1) Run your own Warrior Special Offers. Check Warrior Special Offers section of The Warrior Forum for current rules/restrictions. Email your list if you have one, irrespective of how small, when you launch your WSO. If you have no list, at least mention it on your forum or blog.

(2) If you are a member of email discussion lists, read though a few recent issues and discover a post that you can comment on. Include a *SIG* file as appropriate. This sig file **MUST** include your "Giant Promise." (Note: a *SIG file is an* image *file format created by Broderbund. SIG files hold images used for signs or posters in a proprietary format. SIG files can be opened and edited by Broderbund graphics software, such as PrintShop and Print Master. SIG files cannot be opened on non-Broderbund software, but can be converted to* JPEG *form using an image converter).*

(3) Look through your log files to see which pages are getting the most traffic! Consider putting temporary ads across the tops of those pages.

(4) Edit any of your sites where you have advertisement (such as across the top of a forum) and change those ads to your *Cash $1000 in 24 Hours From The Internet &* add your banner and your Giant Promise.

(5) Email online friends with whom you have a genuine relationship. Explain both what you are trying to accomplish (and why) and also ask them directly for the order.

(6) Change your email signature file to include your latest promotion and **Giant Promise**.

(7) Register as a "show host" and set up and post to your blog at http://BlogTalkRadio.com Search engines are Fond of this platform.

(8) Register at FaceBook.com and set up your own group - specifically centered around your new product. Start following others on Facebook, and as you get noticed, you will quickly develop a following.

(9) Invite each of your followers to join your Facebook group. This allows you to send messages directly to group members via the Facebook platform. You are in-effect *building lists* on Twitter and Facebook, but under no circumstances refer to them that way. The sites are all about social networking, but since you can easily get your message in front of them, this can actually be even more powerful than building a list.

(10) Run a sale – call it your big sale. If you have a product of your own that you've been selling for a while but sales are not moving along, run a sale where you offer the product at deep discount. If the product is a quality product, that should generate some immediate cash flow.

Once you have created a few banners that include your

"Giant Promise," use those banners on forums that allow it. Make sure your banners not only have a URL and title but also an image. Images have been proven to increase your click-through rate, probably because they draw the eye to the link, and spell out a reason to click.

(**Definition: URL** stands for **Uniform Resource Locator**. A URL is a formatted text string used by Web browsers, email clients and other software to identify a *network resource* on the Internet. Network resources are files that can be plain Web pages, other text documents, graphics, or programs).

When you have a desire to generate cash for a specific project and when you are committed to staying debt free; you will be driven to use your creativity and passion to create niche products.

Acknowledge that you may need to stay up 24 hours just doing forum marketing, and building a following on Twitter, if necessary, but that you can do it. Burn the midnight oil if necessary so that you are visible in copious places.

You simply have to get into action.

> *"What you get by achieving your goals is not as important as what you become by achieving your goals."*
> ~Goethe

Step 7 - Your Ultimate Marketing Plan

Three Successful Marketing Tools

(1) My experience teaches me that one of the simplest setups for marketing a report is to use Sid Hale's Rapid Action Profits script.

See the following Link:
http://www.rapidactionprofits.com

I like reworking Private Label Rights products as the products that I sell using Rapid Action Profits because they are so readily available.

(2) If you don't have a lot of free, Private Label Rights products, simply ask on Twitter or Warrior Forum for a recommendation for free giveaways with great gifts. You'll find several that have Private Label Rights products in them. You want to download these with the intention of reusing them immediately.

The method of reworking Private Label Rights products and then marketing them as new products works very well. I see several marketers earning 4-figure and 5-figure incomes each month, and that's the only thing that they really do. The important thing to remember is to make the product your own voice and add value to it. Remember, Private Label Rights products are free, so many people will be recycling them. Make sure yours is better than the rest. Go that extra mile to earn the best results possible. If you have followed me this far, you will see that these are simple steps to quickly creating a product and then getting it into the marketplace. It is only a matter of deciding you are going to do it and then just do it.

(3) Here is one other way to QUICKLY get a product created. Visit any top forum in your niche, identify the thought leaders, or people everyone seem to revere, and simply email them, asking if you can interview them. Decide on the message that you want to get into the market place. Most thought leaders will agree to giving you an interview.

The majority want to help entrepreneurs. You can record

them right over the phone or via Skype. I prefer to use AudioAcrobat. http://www.audioacrobat.com

So now that you now have enough to get into action! You need to stop thinking, stop reading, and start doing. It may seem like a daunting task, but once you get started you'll be amazed at how fast things flow. If you need to take a break from time to time, do so, but commit to not stopping completely until your product is finished, and *out there in the market place.*

Will you earn $1000 or even better in 24 hours? It is up to you. The size of your return is based on how much of yourself you investment in product. You get what you put in. If you read this guide and do nothing you will have wasted your $7. There are too many people who assume that they will generate cash by reading and then doing nothing. Take action by following these steps and you will generate cash.

I have taken you by the hand through the seven easy steps in this guide. This knowledge, along with the confidence that you too can generate cash from the Internet will earn you success. Do not wait to strike till the iron is hot.

Conclusion

In step 1, I have shown you how to scan online forums to identify people's pain and produce a product to solve their pain.

In step 2, I have clearly outlined the reason for testing the market. Trying to sell unwanted products is the biggest mistake I see people make in this business.

In step 3, I have demonstrated how to develop your product quickly by starting with a Private Label Rights product and how to build your list. Remember the money is in the list.

In step 4, I have shown you how to create your "Giant Promise" and unlock the door to product success.

In step 5, I have shown you how to promote your product with my **7 Plan Quick Marketing System™**

In step 6, I focused your attention on sustainability of your product in the market place by **Product Sustainability Marketing 10 Tips™**

Finally, in step 7, the focus is on Message, Market and Media. **Your Ultimate Marketing Plan.**

Take Your First Step and Start

"Desire is the starting point of all achievement, not a hope, not a wish, but a keen pulsating desire which transcends everything." ~Napoleon Hill

I would like to hear of your success. You may contact me, Neslyn Watson-Druée, at contactbeaconpotential@gmail.com

Follow me on Twitter @beaconod

I wish you success in your business and I send you unconditional love and support in all your power and radiant magnificence.